Mechanic Mike's Machines

Submarines

A+

Smart Apple Media

Published by Smart Apple Media, an imprint of Black Rabbit Books
P.O. Box 3263, Mankato, Minnesota 56002
www.smartapplemedia.com

Produced by David West Children's Books
6 Princeton Court, 55 Felsham Road, London SW15 1AZ

Designed and illustrated by David West

Cataloging-in-Publication Data is available from the
Library of Congress.
ISBN 978-1-62588-068-0

Printed in China
CPSIA compliance information: DWCB15CP
311214

9 8 7 6 5 4 3 2 1

Mechanic Mike says:
This little guy will tell you something more about the machine.

Find out what type of engine drives the machine.

Discover something you didn't know.

Is it fast or slow? Top speeds are provided here.

How many crew or people does it carry?

Get your amazing fact here!

Contents

Drebbel

In 1602, the first-ever submarine made a journey down the River Thames in England. It was named the *Drebbel*. Witnesses say it stayed submerged for three hours.

The DREBBEL

The two rowers could not see where they were going. They probably used a compass to navigate.

Did you know that the copy of the *Drebbel* was successfully rowed underwater in 2001?

The *Drebbel* moved very slowly because it was powered by oars. It went to a depth of only 15 feet (4.6 m).

The *Drebbel* was rowed by a crew of two.

The *Drebbel* was human-powered. It had fins at both the front and back and a rudder to steer with.

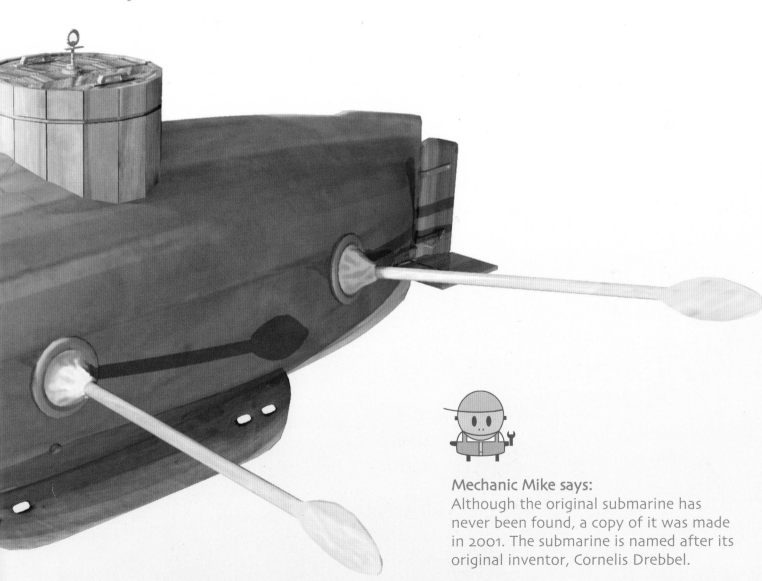

Mechanic Mike says:
Although the original submarine has never been found, a copy of it was made in 2001. The submarine is named after its original inventor, Cornelis Drebbel.

5

Mechanic Mike says:
The *Turtle*'s pilot used a screw on top of the submarine to attach explosives to the bottoms of warships.

The Turtle

The *Turtle* was the first submarine used in war. It was built in 1775 by the Americans during the Revolutionary War. It was designed to attach explosives to the bottoms of enemy warships. Several attempts were made, but all of them failed.

The *Turtle* was sunk by the British navy as it sat onboard an American ship.

The *Turtle* traveled at the speed of a slow walking pace.

Did you know that *Turtle* pilot Ezra Lee was congratulated by George Washington for his brave attempts? Later he became a spy.

There was room for only one person inside the *Turtle*.

The *Turtle* had no engine. The propellers were hand cranked by the pilot.

Holland 1

Holland 1 was the first submarine in the UK's Royal Navy. It was built in secret in 1901 to the designs of Irish engineer John Holland.

The *Holland 1* used a gasoline engine while on the surface and an electric motor when it was underwater.

The *Holland 1* had a crew of eight people.

The *Holland 1* could travel underwater at 7 knots (8.1 miles per hour or 13 km/h).

The *Holland 1* carried two torpedoes. A torpedo is fired from a tube in the submarine. It is powered by a propeller and explodes when it hits its target.

Did you know the *Holland 1* sank in 1913? It was recovered in 1982 and put on display in the UK.

Midget Sub

These small submarines were operated by crews of one or two people. Mother ships normally launched and recovered them. Midget subs were ideal for getting into enemy ports secretly.

Mechanic Mike says:
This midget sub was called a Biber, which is German for beaver. It was the smallest submarine in the German navy during World War II.

10

 A Biber carried two torpedoes on the outside.

A Biber could only manage 5.3 knots (6 miles per hour or 9.8 km/h) when submerged.

 A Biber was operated by one crew member.

 Did you know that although 324 Biber submarines were built, they sank very few ships?

 A Biber used a gasoline engine while on the surface and an electric motor when it was submerged.

U-Boat

During World War II, submarines were used with great success, especially by Germany. Submarines called U-boats hunted in groups, or "wolfpacks." U-boat torpedoes sunk almost 3,000 ships.

Mechanic Mike says:
When attacking a ship, a submarine would lie just under the surface. The captain could see the target through a periscope. This tall tube with mirrors inside could rise above the waves.

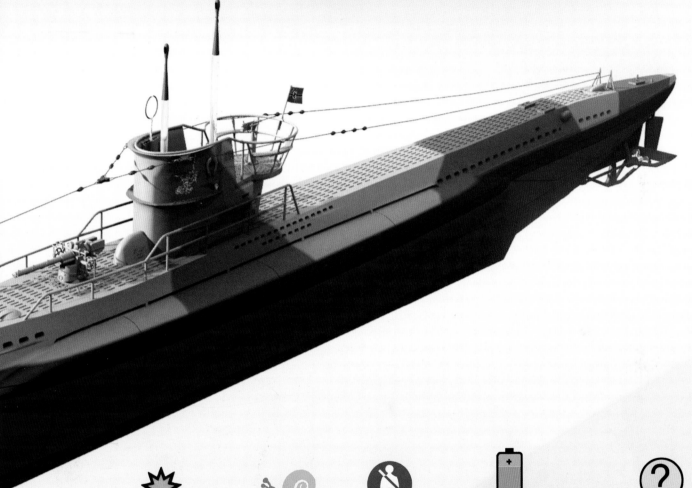

U-boats could only dive to a depth of around 750 feet (230 m). Any deeper and the water pressure would crush the hulls.

This Type VII U-boat could travel at 7.6 knots (8.7 miles per hour or 14.1 km/h) when submerged.

Type VII U-boats had a crew of 44 to 52 men.

Two diesel engines powered the U-boat on the surface. When submerged it used electric motors powered by batteries.

Did you know that underwater submariners could not see where they were going? Instead they used echolocation, known as **SONAR**, to "see" objects underwater.

Nautilus

USS *Nautilus* (SSN-571) was the world's first operational nuclear-powered submarine. Launched in 1954, USS *Nautilus* broke many records for submarine travel. It was taken out of service in 1980.

Mechanic Mike says:
In 1958 the USS *Nautilus* was the first submarine to travel across the Arctic Ocean beneath the ice.

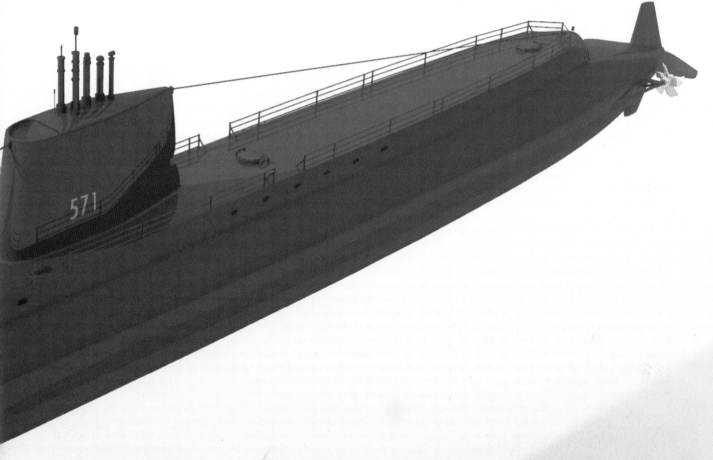

In 1955 the USS *Nautilus* made the longest submerged cruise by any submarine at that time. It covered around 1,100 nautical miles (1,300 miles or 2,100 km).

USS *Nautilus* could reach speeds of more than 20 knots (23 miles per hour or 37 km/h).

USS *Nautilus* had a crew of 13 officers and 92 enlisted men.

Did you know that the hull of *Nautilus* vibrated so much that sonar became ineffective at a speed of more than 4 knots (4.6 miles per hour or 7.4 km/h)?

The USS *Nautilus* was the first submarine to be powered by a **nuclear reactor** to make steam to power **turbines**.

15

Ballistic Missile

Submarines are very difficult to locate, especially when they turn off their propellers and go into silent mode. Navies around the world use nuclear-powered submarines as secret launch pads for missiles with nuclear warheads. These are called ballistic missile subs.

Mechanic Mike says:
This Ohio-class ballistic missile sub can launch its missiles from underwater.

PROJ
41
40

Sub

Submarines equipped to launch Submarine-Launched Ballistic Missiles (SLBMs) are known as "boomers."

The Ohio-class sub can travel at 25 knots (29 miles per hour or 46 km/h) when it is submerged.

Did you know the only thing that limits the time spent submerged is the food supply? The longest patrol is 105 days!

The Ohio-class sub carries 15 officers and 140 enlisted crew members.

These submarines use a nuclear reactor to power the turbines that provide power for the propeller.

Attack Sub

These submarines are designed to attack enemy submarines and ships as well as land targets. They use torpedoes and cruise missiles launched from forward **silos**.

Mechanic Mike says:
Attack subs are difficult to hear because they use special electronics and hull material to remain hidden. Like other submarines, they use SONAR to see where they are going.

This Virginia-class attack sub uses a water jet rather than propellers. The water jet is quieter.

Did you know that submarines carry compressed air so that when they want to rise to the surface they can fill their **ballast tanks** with air? They let the air out to dive.

Its top speed is more than 25 knots (29 miles per hour or 46 km/h). It can dive to around 1,600 feet (490 m).

The Virginia-class attack sub has 14 officers and 120 enlisted crew members.

A nuclear reactor powers a turbine that powers the water jet.

Mechanic Mike says:
This famous submersible is called *Alvin*. It was involved in the exploration of the wreckage of RMS *Titanic* in 1986. RMS *Titanic* sank in 1912 after hitting an iceberg while crossing the North Atlantic on her first voyage.

Submersible

Submersibles are used for underwater **archaeology**, ocean exploration, repairing things, and adventure. They can reach depths far greater than military submarines.

To withstand water pressure at great depths, the crew sits in a 2-inch-thick (5.1-cm) metal sphere.

Alvin can dive to 2.8 miles (4.5 km). It travels at only 2 knots (2.3 miles per hour or 3.7 km/h).

There is room in the metal sphere for two scientists and one pilot.

Alvin uses electric motors to power its thrusters.

Did you know that the deepest dive by a submersible was made in 2013 by James Cameron in *Deepsea Challenger*? It dived to 6.8 miles (11 km) deep in an undersea valley called the Mariana Trench.

Diving Suit

Some modern diving suits are like mini submersibles. They are made out of metal to withstand the water pressure. They are used for work on ocean drilling rigs, pipelines, and sunken ships.

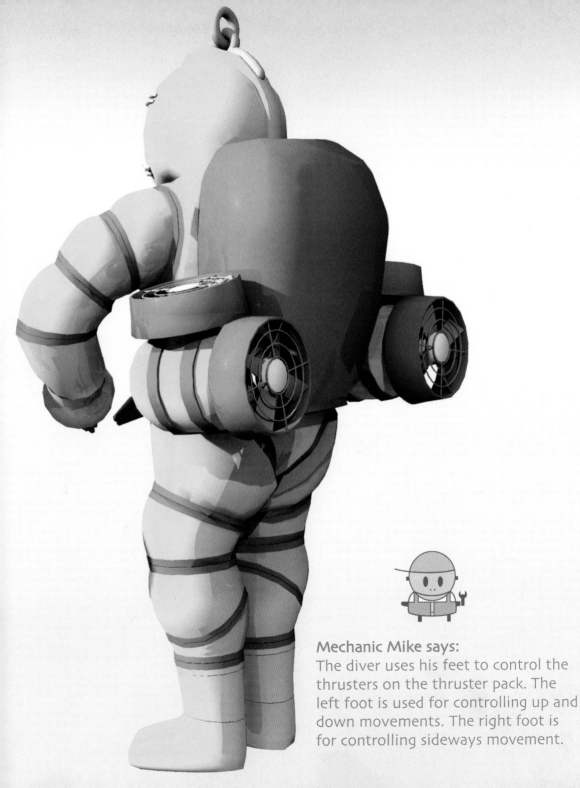

The diver can walk and move his arms because the suit is jointed. The suit has a pair of claws that the diver uses to hold things.

These diving suits can be used to a depth of 1,000 feet (305 m).

Pressurized diving suits are made for one operator.

The thruster pack uses two electric motors to power the propellers.

Did you know that although the divers work in these suits for a few hours the suit can supply enough oxygen for more than two days?

Mechanic Mike says:
The diver uses his feet to control the thrusters on the thruster pack. The left foot is used for controlling up and down movements. The right foot is for controlling sideways movement.

23

Glossary

archaeology
The study of history and prehistory through the excavation of sites.

ballast tank
Tanks in a sub that can be filled with air or water to make it float or sink.

nuclear reactor
A device that uses nuclear fuels to create heat.

silo
A tube that holds one or more missiles.

SONAR
A way of seeing under water by using echo location (**SO**und **N**avigation **A**nd **R**anging).

turbine
An engine which uses gases to rotate blades.

Index